ONE MIND

To The Body
Poems by Maèva Renaud

ISBN 978-0-557-07432-7

FOREWORD

Back in 2004, I was inspired to write a spoken word piece to enter in the New Year. I didn't know what was to become of the piece but it was a foreshadowing to what the Lord planned to do with me and my writing. The piece went like this;

"Window
To
My

soul

Lord
Let
Your

Light

Shine

t h r o u g h

the
Window
To
My

soul.

As *this*

New Year

begins

I
can only think of today
And
how to seek your face
With a true heart
Let me take part

of this **fast**

Consecrating myself unto THEE

Not

allowing my own selfish desires to lead
Lord God today is the day

I

turn

to

You.

With
a willing heart and mind
Show me the way

As I seek

your kingdom first
then all things shall come my way
That which you have ordained
Lord God
I fast
not for my own gain
But for the true followers of Christ
to

come forth

And

e   n   d   u   r   e

the

pain

&

joy

This

New

Year

b   r   i   n   g   s

Lord God
I fast
not for my own gain
But for seekers of Truth
that are

Lost

in their own way
And that by

faith,

wisdom,

knowledge and

understanding

Shall
bring
about

c h a n g e

Father
God
I pray
that as I
seek your face
You
give me strength
to withstand the enemy's tricks
Help me
to detect
Let me not be deceived
Give me provisions
that I may proceed
In my walk with Christ
That others may see your

Light

At work
That they too may be encouraged.
Sanctify me
purify me
And lead me
in the path of righteousness

For **In You** **through You** and
I may go on
not to survive in this land
But to reign as Christ heir in
Heaven
Forever and ever

Amen."

It wasn't until after I shared the piece with my fellow poets that I realized that God was leading me to proclaim a fast, and it was confirmed when I was in my studies of the prophet Joel, where it states, " Blow the trumpet in Zion, consecrate a fast, call a sacred assembly" (Joel 2:15). I went to the Lord and declared that this fast I was proclaiming was not for my own gain but for my family and friends who don't even know the Lord's name, that His will be done and that they too could be saved. I remembered praying (I remembered only because God gave me a unique way to talk to Him through writing) "Lord, I bring this fast to you today; I pray that I do not break it. I pray that this fast is pleasing to your sight and that it brings me closer to you. Direct me on this fast dear Lord, Amen". When I consecrated this fast before the Lord, I had no idea that He had greater and mightier things set before me.

In this fast, I listed some guidelines for myself in my journal which included, keep the Sabbath holy, pray without ceasing, seek God's face, keep away from selfish desires, be mindful for others and let the words that come out of my mouth be the truth. These guidelines weren't easy but they helped me to stay focus, especially when it came to my speech. As a spoken word artist and poet, I use a lot of words. But I didn't want to speak of foolish things, nor did I want to flatter anyone with clever ideas or enticing stories. I wanted to speak the T-R-U-T-H Truth.

A minister from my church, Sister Yvette Staubs, spoke to us one day about the way we speak and the things we say. She mentioned that we should always THINK before we speak, and she broke it down for us with this acronym:
T- if it's not the TRUTH don't say it, H- if it's not HELPFUL don't say it, I- if its not INSPIRING don't say it, N- if it's not NECESSARY don't say it, and K- If it's not KIND don't say. That message gave me a whole new perspective on speaking as well as what I put in my mind to *think* on.

Throughout the fast, my relationship with my Heavenly Father grew more and more as He filled me with His understanding. My drive to be in His word accelerated and my writing became frequent. This went on for a good while until something in my personal life affected me. At the time I did not recognize that the enemy was on my tail for He knew where God was leading me. However, I'm thankful that I serve a God whose faithful promises are my armor and protection because in the midst of my sorrow He lifted me up; out of my weaknesses He made me strong. My spiritual vitality became alive once more as if I had an overdose of Holy Spirit Juice.

I became fervent again, on some sort of long lasting adrenaline rush. I wanted people to know more about my God, more about Jesus and not just by book knowledge but how I knew God. I know God! Yes, Maèvaromynathalie Guirand Renaud knows God. And it hurts me so much to see people in the world who don't know Him or understand Him or choose not to believe in God. It hurt so much that I began to understand why God came to this earth as Jesus and sacrificed himself for our salvation; deliverance and restoration. God longs to be with His people, and He proved that by dying on the cross.

The Lord was really stirring up something inside me because I started seeing things I've never seen before, things I wrote weren't from my own mind, people I met were prophesying over me and prayer became more verbal (I usually wrote to God). I knew God was doing something in me but I didn't understand. He kept calling me to Him, calling me to separate myself from the things of this world. I didn't understand because I thought I did that already. As I seeked His understanding, He told me that I hadn't completely surrendered my life to Him. He told me that there is more to this Christian walk and that I needed to push myself out of my comfort zone. He asked me, out of the 86,000 seconds out of the day, was I living out my faith?

There I was a 21 year old single black female in the ministry, always surrounded by people of the like mind. Using the gifts and talents that the Lord gave me for His Kingdom and God said there is more to it? What else is there Lord? I asked, and He responded,

" *How many of you really love me? You say it with your mouth, but your heart is in doubt. Do you feed my sheep? Do you tend my flock?*"

I felt so ashamed; so unfaithful. But the Lord took that burden away and showed me that His love for me is unfailing. He called me to His word Acts 22:14-15 which states, *"The God of our ancestors has chosen you to know His will and to see the Righteous One and hear Him speak. You are to take His message everywhere, telling the whole world what you have seen and heard"*. I wasn't in a hurry after I read this, but I continued to read the Holy Scriptures. And as I read, God spoke to me more and more about living out my faith and carrying out my duty. I prayed and asked the Lord when, where and how because I knew that if I went out in my own strength, I would be powerless; especially since we battle not against flesh and blood but against powers and principalities. As I continued in scripture I began to question why the church I attended did not teach on such things as spiritual warfare. One thing that the Lord has shown me was that there is a lack of oneness in the body of Christ, a lack of understanding and a lack of surrendering to the Holy Spirit. I became very attentive to reading His word because now I needed solid food. I no longer needed milk; too much milk would have put me to sleep. As I read, I was invoked to write. Writing became so demanding on my part that I didn't want to write anymore, but the Holy Spirit lead me and gave me strength to stay awake and strength for my fingers not to cramp up.

One day, I was lead to write a letter to the leaders of the congregation I attended on the questions I asked the Lord about the body of Christ as a whole (the letter is included in this book). Due to the content of my letter, it was forwarded to the masses of the church members. My letter caused a lot of controversy within my congregation, which was not my intent. I simply wanted my questions answered; I wanted understanding to the things, which were happening to me and to the things that I was seeing with my own eyes. As the days went by a few people came to me and encouraged me to speak up, some didn't understand and some questioned my authority. I had no authority but I learned that when God speaks I must obey. There has been plenty of time when I didn't and I was held accountable. The following week, I was invited to a bible study with one of the sisters from church that encouraged me about my letter. I brought along with me my best friend who came down for the summer from college and my God

I tell you that the Holy Spirit took control of the entire evening. My best friend, who is a Christian, was delivered from several evil spirits that tormented her for years. This was my very first encounter of spiritual warfare and the supernatural. That experience made me realize that God is doing something in the Church, forget just me. But He is calling out His prayer warriors, His demon killers, and His faithful followers. He is calling us out. He has given us the power and authority over all the power of the enemy.

My writings became longer and more potent even to myself. I began writing psalms, letters and speeches. I didn't understand why, but then it was confirmed that the Lord filled me with the spirit of David, Paul and the prophet Jeremiah who was known as the weeping prophet. As the Lord showed me what would happen to his people if they didn't change their evils ways I became distraught. I cried in my sleep for this generation. I asked the Lord, what could I do? People won't listen to me. They look at me and see a fool. They look at me and see a child; they look at me and see an entertainer. I have no degree in theology or religious doctrine, I didn't attend seminary school, and heck I hadn't even completed my undergraduate degree in Film and Television yet. Lord, how can your people listen to me and accept me?

Then I was lead to read the Apostle Paul's letter to Timothy and God spoke to me saying, "*The Holy Spirit speaks to us, in the last times some will turn away, they will follow lying spirits and teachings that come from demons. These teachers are hypocrites and liars. They pretend to be religious but their consciouses are dead. Spend your time and energy in training yourself for spiritual fitness. You are ready to work hard and suffer much in order that people will believe the Truth, for your hope is in the living God who is the savior of all people and particularly to those who believe. Teach these things and insist that everyone learn them. Don't let anyone think less of you because you are young. Be an example to all believers in what you teach, the way you live and in your love, faith and purity. Focus on reading the scriptures to the Church, encourage them and teach them. Do not neglect the spiritual gift you received through the prophecies spoken to you, give your complete attention to these matters. Throw yourself into your task so that everyone will see your progress. Keep a close watch on yourself and on your teaching, stay true to what is right and God will save you and those who hear you. Do not participate in the sins of others keep yourself pure. Don't let the lack of funds prevent you from being rich in actions. Pursue a godly life along with faith, love, perseverance and gentleness. Fight the good fight for what we believe, hold tightly to the eternal life that God has given you. Guard what God has entrusted to you; avoid godless, foolish conversations with those who oppose you with so-called knowledge. Fan into flames the spiritual gift God gave you, for God did not give us the spirit of fear and timidity, but of power, love and self-discipline. So you must never be ashamed to tell others about our Lord. With the strength God gives you be ready to suffer for the proclamation of the Good News.*"

At this point, God called me to a 40 day fast. I've never done a 40 day fast before without food and water. The Lord spoke and said to me that I will hunger for Him and I will thirst for Him. This is what He has been preparing me for from the beginning of the year. When I wrote that spoken word poetry piece, it wasn't for the fast that I proclaimed on my own, it was for the 40 day fast that the Lord called me to. I spoke to no one about my 40 day fast except those who were close to me spiritually. It is so amazing because now I felt like I had no idea how to fast but when it's from God, He orders your steps. I was lead to one of my trusted friends' house one evening and I had an interesting discussion with his mother who was preparing to travel to a conference by the End Time Handmaidens ministries. She provided me with a book called "Your Appointment With God- A Bible Study on Fasting" by Gwen Shaw. This piece of motivational literature was definitely an inspiration from God himself. It elevated my mind to a better understanding of prayer and fasting and it is a very instrumental source for the body of Christ. I would recommend this publication to anyone who wants to know more about God, their faith, their calling, prayer and fasting.

As the Lord separated me from my day job, school and friends, He began to reveal things to me about myself, things that needed change. I'm the type of person that likes to be in control especially when it comes to my work. But the Lord showed me that this characteristic trait needed to die. Maèva needs to die. As He continued to strip me of my ambitions, my goals, my dreams, my desires, I began to understand why. In his word, He said that all things shall pass away. Everything I've ever desired, everything I planned to do in my future as a writer, poet, actress, dancer, producer, is all vanity. I was living a life of pure vanity. Nothing really matters, for when our Lord and Savior returns, the only thing that matters is our faith.

I am so grateful for the ones who planted a seed in my life and more for those who watered it. If it wasn't for their obedience to God and fulfilling the duty they were called to do, I would have never been saved and they would have been held accountable when judgment time comes. That is why I know now that there is more to Sunday Morning Church service, Sunday evening service, Monday evening women's group, Tuesday night praise and worship practice, Wednesday night bible study, Friday night youth group and Saturday Morning prayer. There is more to this routine, there is a world out there that the Church has closed its doors to. People of the world aren't going to Church. They'd rather spend Sunday mornings at Barnes & Nobles or starbucks or grocery shopping or at the beach. As Christians, we need to go to these people and proclaim the gospel of Jesus Christ to them. They aren't going to come to us, the Church must go to them. That is what God is preparing His soldiers for. To go out to all nations, making them disciples and baptizing them in the name of the Lord Jesus Christ, teaching them all the things that God commanded.

We are living in the end times, the last generation before the rapture. People need to know, people need to understand, that's the plague, which destroys us now-lack of knowledge, True knowledge that comes from God. He is calling His people to repentance, for there is forgiveness of sins for all who turn to Jesus.
Repent I say and save yourselves from this wicked generation. I now know what I must do; For the Lord has called me to be His disciple. That is what my fast is all about. He is preparing me for a dangerous mission, a mission to tell everyone about the coming of the Kingdom of God.

As you read this please be in prayer for the hearts of those who hear the message I must bring. Pray for the deliverance of those in bondage, pray for the healing of the sick, pray for unity in the body of Christ and pray that one day you and I will rejoice together in our Father's Kingdom.

Glory to God for the ability to formulate thoughts into words that people can read and understand. My life is worth nothing unless I use it for doing the work assigned to me by the Lord Jesus, the work of telling others the Good News about God's wonderful kindness and love.

Included in this book are poems, letters and songs that have helped me in my walk with Christ. Everything you've read and will read is either straight from scripture, inspiration from God or God Himself. After reading this book, you will definitely notice and understand where I have been, and where God is taking me. I pray that you be encouraged in your walk with Christ and allow God to continually cleanse your heart and renew your mind.

I can only be what He called me to be,
Maèva

Dedicate To My Little Brother Kenny,
I started for you, may you find God's love and salvation.
I love you.
- Na

CONTENTS

Survival of the Lost Stone
Poems written from 1999- 2000

Prologue

Sent to do nothing
Is that why I'm here?
To do nothing
My whole solitary life
What have I accomplished?
Did I find the cure to aids?
Did I find a natural resource?
Am I making this world a better place for you or me?

Why Am I HERE?
What is my purpose?
Do I bring happiness to someone's eye?
Do I care about the world?
Do I love you? Do you love me? Do I love me?

What's going on around here?
What the hell is going on?
I'm Lost

Alone

Why do I feel so lonely?
Like something is missing inside
Sometimes my heartaches
I feel alone and lost
I just want someone in my life
Someone to love and care
And hold me tight
Some one I can trust
And tell all my secrets to
Someone who will be there for me even when I fall
Someone with a helping hand
Someone who will wipe my tears away
Someone who will comfort me
Someone who'll love me for me
Is that too much to ask?

Birth of A Stone
Bizarre questions come to mind.
Knowing there are no correct answers
Lost and Dazed.
Scientist have a theory—Man evolved from apes!
Do I defy what was brought upon me?
Did God create man?
Thoughts cluster my mind.
Knowledge I have obtained turns into questions.
Question? Is having a college degree make you educated?
Question? Is knowing what others don't make you wiser?
What have I learned so far?
Question? Is the " system" up to something?
How can a race that needs each other to survive
Kill one another for material things?
A generation who are known to be corrupted
Who corrupted us???
Aren't we the future?
Or are we just living the past with special effects?
Question? Is it right to care for people who think of you as a disgrace?
Is it my fault to love someone and not be loved?
Question? Is asking too many questions wrong?
Why is trying to communicate with someone
To become together as one so difficult?
Questions cluster my mind all the time
Causing tremendous headaches
Why are things so confusing?
Why can't I get one simple answer?
Does God make it this way for us to find out on our own?
If that's how it is no wonder I'm lost.
But this is just the beginning of my journey
I know there will be more questions
But I'll find the Answer.
The One Answer.

The Plague

In my mind I wonder
How well do we know ourselves?
Our worlds
I myself am confused
Of the definition of self
It doesn't really help me to
Overstand the real meaning of one's self
       You know what I mean
And I figure
For me to know
I must journey on about into the world
And see how I myself
Handles it
But
Look at our world
We live in a society where people claim
To love the Almighty
But go on hating, discriminating, killing
Sinning
May I go on?
We live in "Da Mans" world
It's true
Some people are blind or afraid to see what's going on
You see all the oppression going on
All the hatred
Civil rights movement?
Who killed X & King?
Now they've got Jesse and Powell
Wrapped around their fingers
Whatever happened to the
Reincarnated Nat Turner?
It's the millennium time for a change
A new and improved revolution
We want revolution
But most of the cats
Don't know revolution
I'm tired of problems keeping me pessimistic
Emancipation Proclamation
Freed the slaves but ain't free our minds
We still got that nigga mentality
You brainwashed us with Bill of Rights
Which will be used against me in the court of law
Who makes these laws?
Whose world is it?

Mine?
Am I out my cotton pickin' mind
Maybe so but I never picked cotton
Never will
My voice will be heard
To the extreme
If I have to bleed for it
Let it be
On your dollars it says "In God we trust"
You don't even know Him
The Almighty
Money doesn't faze Him
He cares for truth
The heart the pure heart
Not hypocrisy and negligence
He loves with closed eyes
All His children
He helps us
Guides us and nurtures us
I need you Lord
To help me and guide me
To search for truth
Help me overstand your plan
Quench my thirst Lord
Help me find my way home
Help me and my people Lord
We are being washed away
Not by your tears
But by the oppression
This Plague
We call society.

The Journey

Life
I have many questions about that four-letter word
I noticed a lot of my thoughts
Have changed
They are more deep mental notes
Spiritual natural vibrations
The new me
My new format MakedaCiph
However I will not forget my past.
My future is what is in front of me.
And that's what I'm looking onto.
But first I must find myself
Myself as in my cipher
My soul
LostOne, that is who I am
Not lost in the world
But the world in me
I must go and find my world
360 the circle of my life
Right now I confuse many
That come about
But I like it that way
Let the world try to decipher me
LostOne always to be
MakedaCiph
I'm going on a quest
To search my spirit, my soul
To see if this is where my roots really are
I have a lot on my mind
People say I think too much
But I am who I am
Am I?
Someone once said
This is my life
This is what I know
This is who I am
There's no more to it.

Caught Up

Caught up in between
Two of the unseen
Difficult to explain
Difficult to choose
To choose just one
But what is one?
Can one be all that I need?
Deep down I can't imagine
The thought of two
However I do not want to lose
Either one
No heads or tails
This is a decision
But how can you make a decision
On something so involuntary
So incomplete
So vague
I need to analyze and strategize
My thoughts
Level it out
Figure out
The truth and nothing but the truth
But don't mislead or mistreat
Be alert and distinguish
What the outcomes are
Look deep down into your soul
What is it that you want?
Is that what you want?
Don't confuse yourself Maeva
Be realistic
Paper or Plastic

The Answer

I found something
It's kind of hard to explain
But I found something
That makes perfect sense
This magnificent Thing
Is the Answer
To all my questions
Why didn't I see it before?
Was I so blind in the world?
So lost in society
The Answer
Was right in the palm of my hands
I am shocked
The Answer
Was with me all along
I just didn't accept it
But I do now
I do now
You are the Answer Jesus
And I accept you
I accept you in my heart
In my life
I accept You

Changed

To know and to believe
Are two different things
Knowing something is sure
Is totally different from believing it.
There was a time when I thought
My world was all over
My life was just a mistake
I put my all in too many worldly things
I thought I could be happy
With just friends, family and myself
But happiness came and went
Love was just used up like water
I didn't know where I was going
Why I was here
It was all like a bad dream
A dream I wanted to end
Forever
And one day
I met somebody
Somebody that knows everybody
And this Somebody told me
He can handle it
Don't be afraid anymore
I am here for you
Just put your trust in Me
And you'll be saved
And that's the day
My whole life
Changed

About time I told you

Let me tell you 'bout the time
I told you that I loved you
Everything came from my heart
So pure and so true
Lord I need you in my life
To help me keep from fallin'
Everyday and every night
That's why I keep on callin'
Lord Jesus
Father God I pray
That you forgive me of my sins
Father God I pray that you
Keep your spirit
Within me
Lord I know you died for me
Right there on Calvary
The sweetest thing you did for me
Is give your life so willingly
So here I am before you
A sinner yes its true
But now my life belongs to you
To do the work you want me to
Lord Jesus
Everyday and every night
Now I'm gonna tell you why
I'm a say it
Ain't no lie
My God My God My God
My God is true
My God is right
My God is there with me
Through my painful nights
He brings me joy
When I'm sad
He gives me comfort
Until I'm glad.

Armstrong Fever

I see the light blue sky
And rays of bright sunlight
Breathe the fresh new air
And let the breeze massage my face
Humming birds in the air
Sweet melodic voices
Down yonder music is heard
I think to myself
What a wonderful world
Now is it
Tell me really is it
People dying everywhere
Sistahs used and abused
Brothas locked up
Chirren' glocked up
Gotta stay strapped up
To survive in this land
Controlled by da man
You control our lifestyles
But not our Christ style
Living the inner city blues
Where the wise slave
Overcomes the rich fool.

Maximum Capacity

Let Me Recite My Poetry
Express My Feelings
I can't Hold It In NO More
Its Maximum Capacity
My Words Need TO be Heard
From Now to Eternity
You need to hear my news
My knowledge I don't misuse
Thoughts I can't suppress
That stuff
Always had me stressed
Lord I know that I've been blessed
People Say I want to do too much
The way I see it
There's a lot to do
God gave me talents
And I'm a sho'nuff
Put them to use
So let me recite my poetry
Express my feelings
Can't hold it in no more
Its Maximum Capacity.

Psalmist Speaks
Poems From 2002-2003

Lovadastic Blues Revised

Is this love that I'm feelin'
Don't wanna be a sinner no more
Love is the feeling I'm feelin'
Don't wanna play them worldly games no more
It's about time now
That I can get down now
So come on Jesus
Let's get out of town now
Just me and you
Groovin' to
The lovadastic blues
Abba Daddy
I do know
That you the only one for me
So Abba Daddy
Let's get this praise started
Cuz I'm lovin You
Cuz Your love is real
Your love is Pure
Jesus what you got for me is Truth
All I want to do is praise you
Lift You up and hold You high
Cuz Your love is Faithful
Ain't no other God most High
Jesus who
Just saved my life
From everlasting hell
I pray that you take
This praise as a favorable smell
It's just me you
We grooving to
The Lovadastic Blues
Me and you
We keeping cool
Lovin me
Lovin you
Feel so good
Love is real
Love is pure
Daddy what you got for me is Truth.

Have Thine Own Way

Have Thine Own Way
Have Thine Own Way
Have Thine Own Way
Have Thine Own Way with me
When I think about myself
And the things I want to do
Have Thine Own Way
When I wake up in the morning
At the crack of dawn
Have Thine Own Way
Lord I want you to take control
Lord I want you to have my soul
My spirit and my mind
Are no longer mine
Jesus Christ just take control
Jesus Christ just take control
The Devil no longer has a hold on me
Because I've been set free.

Time With You

I just want to spend a little more time with you
Just wanna spend a little more time with you
Just wanna spend a little more time with you Lord

Just wanna spend a little more time
With the One who gave me life
I need to know you more
You're the One that I adore
I need to know you Lord
I need to know you Lord

I just want to spend a little more time with you
Just wanna spend a little more time with you
Just wanna spend a little more time with you Lord

Here in my quiet place
I want to see your face
Lord I'm asking
Lord I'm seeking
Reaching Reaching Reaching
For your grace

I just want to spend a little more time with you
Just wanna spend a little more time with you
Just wanna spend a little more time with you Lord

Spoken Word

Lord I know that I've been changed
I know that I won't be the same as I used to be
Lord ever since you came into my life
Everything has not been the same for me
Lord this change inside of me
Proves to society that you are God
Lord now that I can see
All the things you've done for me
When you died on Calvary
Bearing all of my iniquities
The blood you shed for me
Shows how much you care for me
And now that I'm a new babe in Christ
I give my life to Thee

Lord I know that I've been changed
I know that I won't be the same as I used to be
Lord ever since you came into my life
Everything has not been the same for me
Lord this change inside of me
Proves to society that you are God
You changed my ways you changed my life
Everything you've done for me
Leads to my prosperity
Jesus Christ my Lord
You are whom I'm livin' for
My faith in you My works for you
Helps me to be true
You promised that I would inherit your kingdom
If I keep my mind on Spiritual things
Instead of my fleshly nature
For yes I will stumble and fall
And face my trials and tribulations
For in your Word it says that
All things work together for good
To those who love you
And those that are called to your purpose
For those of you listening
You'll find that first
In Romans Chapter Eight
And further down
It talks about who can separate

Us from Christ
Not tribulations or Distress
Nor Persecution or nakedness
Nor Famine nor peril or swords
For yet all these things
I am more than a conqueror
Through Him who loves me
And now I give me live to Thee
As I take heed to this ministry
Which I have received in the Lord
That I may fulfill it
Not for my profit
But to God be the glory
As I speak to you the truths of all truths
Of Christ's' story in form of spoken word
God's Word
Cuz in the beginning was the Word
And the Word was with God
And the Word was God
And God became Flesh
That I may receive Him
And now I am a new Creation
Thanks be to God.

Lord I know that I've been changed
I know that I won't be the same as I used to be
Lord ever since you came into my life
Everything has not been the same for me
Lord this change inside of me
Proves to society that you are God
Lord now that I can see
All the things you've done for me
When you died on Calvary
Bearing all of my iniquities
The blood you shed for me
Shows how much you care for me
And now that I'm a new babe in Christ
I give my life to Thee

Spiritual Vitality

Even when I'm so confused
You guide me on what I need to do
I'm so thankful that I could have
A relationship with you
Sometimes I can be a little
Hard headed but your mercy and grace is sufficient
After I sinned and confessed it.
Lord you care for me so much
I feel that my works for you
Are not enough
I know all you want from me is my heart
But you are so awesome
I want to give you all I've got
Sometimes my actions
Maybe misleading
And my thoughts can be unpleasing
Yeah that devil is deceiving
That's why I need you 24/7
To fill me with your spirit
And help others get to heaven
I try my best to obey your commands
But without you ordering my steps
It's kind of hard to withstand
The blows of society
Misconceptions of Christianity
People just can't quite see
Why they need
The Trinity
But now that I've been set free
The Spirit in Me Speaks
One Father
One Son
One Spirit
Three
In One
Is all I need
I'm not trying to live in bondage with religion
I believe in Jesus Christ
That's what makes me a Christian
Knowing He died for me on Calvary
Should've of been me on that cross you see
With all my sins
He still loves me

And that's why I give my life to THEE
Renewing my spiritual vitality
Pursuing peace with all my brothers and sisters
Regardless what they do
Because Christ loves me
I can love all too
But remember He's watching our every move
So fear the Lord
And all His works
Cuz life without Him
Is like not knowing your own worth.

Verses

Faith comes by hearing
And hearing by the Word of God
For the Word of God is Living
And powerful
Sharper than any two-edge sword
Piercing even to the division
Of spirit and soul
And the joints and marrows
And is a discerner of thoughts and the intents of the heart
But grace and truth come through
Jesus Christ
But as many as received Him
To them He gave the Right to become Children of God
And God became flesh and dwelt among us
In Him was life and the life was the light of men
He opened the door for anyone who wanted to endure
Life abundantly
So now you'll see
Greater things, than these
Says He
Heaven shall open and the angels of God
Ascending and Descending
Upon the Son of man
And in Him I am a new creation
Like a Haitian
Benitsoi Leternel
For the relationship that we have with Him
Giving us the ability to recite scripture
Not to get richer with dollar dollar bills yall
But in the spirit
Cuz man made the money
Money never made the man
But either way all is temporary
So set your sights on Jesus Christ
The One and Only Savior
With the Eternal Flavor
If you don't believe me
Check out them verses.

Worship

I will worship Christ (3x)
With all of my soul
I will worship Christ (3x)
With all of my soul
In Spirit and Truth
I'll worship you
With every inch of my mind
I'll worship Christ
In all of my heart
I'll worship You

A Letter To Hip Hop

I want to thank you for what you've made me become.
Over the years I've kept my head up trying to survive in this penitentiary.
Seemed like you were the only one who understands me.
You taught me not to be blinded by the constant stereotypical views of a black bandit.
Only proclaiming the truths of black struggles in this land and if I ruled the world,
Hip Hop
would be the commander and chief but since I don't,
Hip Hop
will still be the drive and passion instilled in me.
Hip Hop
for you I'd ride and die because
the message you bring is what helps me to survive.
Cuz back in the days when I was young,
Tupac and Biggie was like my moms,
yeah sometimes we argued but you revealed the truths of life and how to get through.
And when the fugees came out with the score,
I was like yeeaah, yall best not be dissin' us refugees no more.
Hip-hop
can you believe we made it this far?
I've grown with you, cried with you, shoot I know I'm gonna die with you.
You know I'm here through thick and thin,
all the times they've been hatin on us, waitin' for us to fall apart.
But our love for the most High God kept us movin on, growin' strong, marchin' on in this
battlefield between limelight and intellectual zeal.
But now I'm getting older and I'm looking closer into your heart,
It looks like we're growin apart
Like a church with fake Christians
Hip-hop
you letting the devil slip in.
What happened to the revolutionary within?
Cuz now it's bigger than hip-hop
When you just tryin to fill yo' pockets with dead prez.
It just saddens me what you've become
Cuz before it was like we were one.
But all you do is hate on me
I can't quite see why the game
Hasn't set you free
Yeah I know life is hard
And you've got to make ends meet
But we did it before

Remember?
That's what you taught me
To be that Brand Nubian Queen
How I could be what I want to be
And now
That I see that you need me
I'm a school you
Like you schooled me
Cuz we can't die now
They not ready
This is a war and we've got madd headz to carry
Hip Hop
I hope you listening
Cuz I'm coming from the heart
I got this pen in my hand thinking
Damn that's where it all starts
Yo Girl forever

Who Am I?

I'm that Soul Sista
Make You Say
"Oh No How She Figga"
Put You Out There
Make You Think
About your Life
'For you gets Extinct
I've been through Trials
And Tribulations
So I know
What its like
MR. FaceMen
You think I don't keep it Real
Cuz I'm a CHRISTIAN
Well Christianity is as REAL as it Gets
Cuz Jesus Christ is the only ONE
Who'll pay your debt
I ain't the # 1 Stunna
But I'm a Runna
In this Race
So I'm a keep seekin
God's Face
Been On this Journey
3yrs Now
Go ahead and Ask Me How
But I'm a tell you Who I AM
That Nappy Headed
Poets Soul
People Lovin
CHRISTIAN

I'm Christian

Yes I know I mess up sometimes
Flesh is weak
And you ain't feelin' my vibe
So Christians –Prayer is all I need
From you instead of ridicule
I know that Jesus saved me
But it's madd hard living a Christian life
It gets crazy
So don't judge, don't scold, don't hate
Just cuz I act this way
My life is my testimony
I praise, I fast, I pray
So don't you mistake
My actions as child's play
We all sin and fallen short
But you know what I adore
Is His mercy, His power, and His grace
Jesus Christ that's whom I put my faith
In cuz He saved my life
From the things I went through and If I told you
You'd want to cry
Hi
I ain't perfect no how no way
My faith in God is what matters to me
Just praisin' Adonai
Is what gets me high
No reffas, no buds, no syzurp
For me to get my spirit stirred up
Naturally I get high, high, high
Off praise dancing, bible reading, tongue speaking
Praise the Lord every single weekend
On Monday and Tuesday too
Wednesday night we meet up at the school
Hold UP
I'm a keep it true
So you could understand my news
I'm Christian- Not cuz I go to church
I'm Christian- Not cuz I read the word
I'm Christian- Not cuz I fast and pray
I'm Christian- Cuz its all about faith
In Christ—now what you say
In Christ—I walk the way
In Christ—I do my thang
In Christ—I keep it tight everyday.

Ayitienne Rebellion

U.S. of A?
    U.S. of A?
        Why you always lying to me?
        Since I came to this country
            Where I'm supposed to be free
            You entrapped me in this police state
                Called "niggahtivity.
            Exploiting my mind with your
            Capitalistic brainwashing
            Shenanigans
        Ever since I was a kid
            You placed me in your mental institutions
            Otherwise known as public schools
            Yeah schooling me to be the best
            That I can be
            In the United States Army?
            Feeding me His-story through your eyes
            Making yourself look good as if you were never at fault.
U.S. of A?
    U.S. of A?
        Why you always lying to me?
        This supposed to be the land of opportunity
        But I can't do nothin'
        Without social security
    Is you keepin' an eye on me
U.S. of A?
        Huh?
U.S. of A?
        My telephones tap, ta, tap-taps
        When I pick it up
    What?
        You checking up on me
        Like X and Huey P.
        Because I have a voice that
        Will reach here to eternity
U.S. of A?
    Can you explain this to me?
        Why do you say that my people are not American?
    Do you not know your own
    Geographical nonsense?
        The West Indies is a part of North America

So I am 100% American
As any other white European immigrant
Who comes into this country
With no trials or tribulations
They don't have to worry about
No health care or being sent back to their own nation
So why?
U.S. of A?
Do you keep lying to me?
This land ain't my land neither is it your land
So stop trying to run us out our own neighborhoods
Jacking up the rent
Fixing up the place so yo folk could move in!
How are we suppose to better ourselves
If you keep labeling us and keeping us divided
Don't you think other Nubians will figure out
What you're up to like I did?
U.S. of A?
I'm getting sick and tired of you lying to me
I see what you do when conflict confronts you
Start a war with another country
Or exile people off sea
Like you did Charlie Chaplin and Isadora Duncan
Were you afraid of their civil statements?
What's there to fear?
U.S. of A?
I see you cling to your purse
When I come near
Why do you follow me when I'm in your stores?
Think I might thief your precious Christian Diors?
And why are you exploiting my sistahs on your tell-lies-vision
As music video whores
Pimping our rappers for your own profit
And quick to lock them up and say rap music is garbage
U.S. of A?
U.S. of A?
Why you always denying us our identity
My people ain't just children of slavery
Yes we come from a land afar
Created by the One who made the moon and the stars
My people may be dark-skinned, light skinned
Caramel or mahogany
But that's the way God made us
Beautiful, fine, to sum it up Unique
See we are all heirs of the kingdom of Christ
So stop filling our heads up

With your filthy demonic lies
I'm just here trying to do my thing
So yall better repent
Cuz lying is a sin.

Learn

You'll learn
When somebody do you wrong
You'll learn
Cuz you acting like you grown—child
You'll learn
By the end of this song
That life ain't easy please believe me
You'll learn

I need to be real with you right now
It really does hurt a lot right now
I don't even know or understand
This pain I feel within right now

It's been a while now
And even though we
Well him and I
Aren't that close anymore
It still hurts

He is here
Right now
In my presence not even having one little inkling of what is going on in my mind or in
my heart
I don't even think he even cares---anymore
Cuz he's happy now
With his love long lost
Happiness is what he seeks
And for a moment I gave him bliss
But now I feel like I've been dissed

You'll learn
When somebody do you wrong
You'll learn
Cuz you acting like you grown—child
You'll learn
By the end of this song
That life ain't easy please believe me
You'll learn

Never before have I encountered such betrayal
If he can act as if nothing happened between us
I want to be able to do that too

But who am I fooling
Something did happen
We happened
From being his buddy buddy friend
To cuddle up close at the drive in
Late night movies
Creating friction
On the couch and
Lip glossin
From lip lockin
Sweet caress
To nakedness
Love explored
But now no more

You'll learn
When somebody do you wrong
You'll learn
Cuz you acting like you grown—child
You'll learn
By the end of this song
That life ain't easy please believe me
You'll learn
For every action
There's a reaction
That craziness you do
Will catch up to you
You'll learn

Confusion has made a score on me
Should of seen it coming
Should of kept on running
The race of life and death
I'm running out of breath
I need some air I need some space
The love in my heart has lost its place

I'm sorry Lord
I know I went on a frenzy
This isn't like me
I don't want to feel no more
The way I do towards---him
It messes up my lifestyle
So please fill me
With your peace and understanding
So I'll learn

You'll learn
When somebody do you wrong
You'll learn
Cuz you acting like you grown—child
You'll learn
By the end of this song
That life ain't easy please believe me
You'll learn
For every action
There's a reaction
That craziness you do
Will catch up to you
You'll learn

You'll learn- brotha
You'll learn- sista
You'll learn – mista
Cuz that mess will bring you down
You need to stay on higher ground
And listen to the sound
From the words up above
It'll bring you so much love
You'll learn

You'll learn
When somebody do you wrong
You'll learn
Cuz you acting like you grown—child
You'll learn
By the end of this song
That life ain't easy please believe me
You'll learn.

Little Girl

Little girl why do you cry?
In a foreign land without a plan
Support system is on hold
Can't function without it
Let the truth be told
Little girl cries
All alone in this faraway place
Dry tears on her cheeks
Remember her first date
With pretty boy blue
Who wanted to screw
He'll rest in peace in his bed tonight
As little girl cries
For someone to care
And scream with her
I hate this place
Little girl why do you cry?
Mama's been gone 16 years
Never did she wipe away the tears
Angry with God
How could you do this?
Left out in the cold
And no one to hold her
Tight
Daddy tries all the time
Role-playing
Mommy but it's not the same
Growing up as a tomboy
Wait a minute could I be gay
Never that
Little girl cries
Tossed to and Fro'
Wanting to wake up out
Of this dream for a better tomorrow
Little girl why do you cry?
Stepmother now
Burned her hair
TCB, Just for me almost left her bare
Locked out the house
Numerous times
Called the cops
Stepmother kids
Stabbed daddy with a knife

Crazy
Little girl runs away
Sitting on a mango tree
Pondering what life would be
If she was not to be
Digging her own grave
But to her dismay
She had a grandmother
Who prayed
Little girl cries to this very day
For If not all the experiences
She would not be hear today
Taking on the challenges of life
As a token on the road
Tossing, flipping
Or just not picking
So why little girl do you still cry?
These tears are tears of joy
Overcoming in this foreign land but now knowing the Master's Plan
Fulfilling the purpose of my being.

True Love Waits

Everybody wants to be loved
But to receive love you must give love
Right
Love?
You say If I really Loved you I would give you some of my-- sweet love
But I don't know what kind of love you talking about cuz my love is --patient
And I sho' nuff won't be deceived
Cuz my intimacy needs to be with --the Word of God
My intimacy needs to be in-- prayer and fasting.
Instead of you asking
Me to rest in peace.
So put away your Trojan horse
Cuz ain't no intercourse going on around here.
Cuz what you want is carnal
What I want is pure
Yes He created us to be fruitful and multiply
But I ain't trying to live no lie
So let's take back what the devil stole
When he turned our love into a feast on flesh
1969 was not a very good year
Are you hearing me my dear?
Love takes time to grow
So let's activate our faith—no not masturbate
But in solitude where He who plants and He who waters are one
So let God put our pieces back together
As He laid you down to sleep to create me for you
And planted His seed deep within that we may reflect Him.

Window To My Soul
Poems From 2004

Window To My Soul

You're looking in
Looking in
Through the window
The window
To my soul
You're looking in
From the cold
Cold world
Being deceived
Not knowing
That you are not free
Living in this illusion
Of what we call society
Being fooled by the
Master of disguise
Not knowing that the life
You're living is a lie
But you keep looking
Looking through the window
To my soul
This world is not what it seems
Please take heed
As the Truth be told
All shall pass away
But the praises
Shall be eternal to the
Most High God
Yahweh
Yahweh is and forever will be
The Light that shines
Through the window
To my soul
But you're just looking
As if you've got some strong hold
Holding you back
From opening my
Window.

4 Letter Words

4 letter words
like WORD
used to speak the truth
used to teach the youth
words with 4 letters
like LIFE
the greatest GIFT
he could ever GIVE
Especially when He gives it to you
Twice
L-I-V-E
Live
I'm alive
In Christ
4 letters set me
FREE
As He chose me
To be His
SEED
4 letter words
brought me on bended knee (PRAY)
When life was like a living HELL
No need to dwell
On my past mistakes
For that's what makes me
Who I am
Today
And I'll keep growing
In Faith
As my life has been changed
4 letter words like
SEEK
FIND
OBEY
Brought my flesh to the grave
And now all I have to say is
HOLY
Is His
NAME

GOS PO E TREE

What you know about that gospoetry
GOS PO E TREE
For if it were not for the tree of life
I wouldn't be here reciting my rhymes
Sometimes they don't
So I can't front
But when the words leak from my pen
It could only come from within
And what's within me
But the Spirit of the One
Who died on Calvary
Now you'll see—why
My poetry shouldn't be labeled
As Floetry or Russell Simmons
Def Poetry
But GOS PO E TREE
Bringing Jesus to the streets
They call me the P.O.E.T
Putting on eternal Truth
Speaking the words of Truth
From Matthew, John and Ruth
And there's even more
Cuz the God that I adore
Gave me a whole book to explore
So now I must endure
The ridicules of the multitudes
Of the devils advocates
But you know what
I know the Lord is one who keeps ordering my steps
Cuz as a child of the Light
Reppin for J. Christ
Spreading eternal life
Forever I'll be a vessel for the Lord
To set you free
This spokenword revolution
What you know about
That GOS PO E TREE?

See You Later Alligator

See you later alligator
After a while crocodile
Don't you know my mind is made up?
I don't need you here no how

You were here for just a moment
But now you gots to get the goin'
So bye bye crocodile

Don't want no more of your kisses
Save them for your other misses
Cuz you ain't sly crocodile

I ain't here to play your fool
There's too much for to do
I don't need you
So bye bye crocodile

Crocodile why you chasing me
I know that you're hating me right now
But I got another lover
Like no other
Loving me oh so good
Crocodile I know you wish you could
But here's what I gotta say

See you later alligator
After a while crocodile
Don't you know my mind is made up?
I don't need you here no how

So bye bye crocodile
So bye bye crocodile

You were never good to me
All you tried to do is use me
And I won't take it no more
So you better get out the door
Cuz I've been changed
I'm not the same
And I ain't playing no more of your games
Cuz I've been changed
I'm not the same

And I ain't playing no more of your games

See you later alligator
After a while crocodile
Don't you know my mind is made up?
I don't need you here no how

Don't let the door hit ya
Where I should of kicked ya
Bye bye crocodile

Letters To The Body

1)
In the midst of my devotional time with God I was inspired to share with you what I learned from John 10:41 " He did no miracles but everything he said about Jesus was true."
So please take this letter to heart, because it's from mine to yours,

John the Baptist was a revolutionary bringing about change in the society he lived in, proclaiming the Truths of the soon to come King and the need for repentance. After his death, memories of his boldness began to fade but people remembered his words. As modern day revolutionaries, I encourage you to continue on in this mission as God prepares you and keeps your steps in order. Through your spoken word, storytelling, praise dancing, rhyme reciting, seeds are being planted. Though' they may seem dormant at times, in due season will beautiful fruit grow. So I say to you S.I.O. members, though' we may not be remembered as the greatest artist, when our time has passed, let us be remembered for speaking the TRUTH.

Our blessings come from Above that we maybe able to spread His Love.

2)
 Isn't it amazing how God can allow us to go through trials and tribulations and in His word He tells us that we should let these trials that we face be an opportunity for joy.

I wondered why He would say that, I mean a lot of these issues and problems we sometimes get ourselves in can really bring us down.

But you know I realized that God, He wants us to endure these trials, He wants us to experience them but not on our own for in His word it states that He would never leave us nor forsake us. He is in the midst of our problems; He is there to help us get through it. That's WHY HE SAID TO BE JOYFUL!

With God in our lives, we don't need to worry about our problems, we can rejoice because God is our refuge; He is our shelter, our protector. He has ordered His angels to protect us from the hands of the enemy.

We don't need to worry about what we are going through, we must rejoice for God is bringing us through it!

He is there, it's not by luck that you were able to get a loan, it's not by luck you were able to get out of that situation, it's not by luck at all. God is Almighty, All Powerful, All knowing, Faithful and Loving.

He created us, we are His children, and He would not leave us out in the cold. He Is GOD; HE IS HERE WITH US, WITH YOU. TRUST HIM AND REJOICE, BE GLAD THAT HE'S ALREADY WORKING OUT YOUR SITUATION.

THE BATTLE IS NOT YOURS BUT THE LORD'S- don't let your experience rid you of your victory. Remember, you are a Child of God, Trust HIM, not the world.

Hallelujah, God is filling your heart right now, thank Him, for this morning, and thank Him for this week. Praise His name for He is worthy. He is worthy! Hallelujah.

Commit yourself to trusting God. He's the only one who would never turn His back on you.
Commit yourself to living for God.
Commit yourself to reading His Holy Word.

I'm so blessed to have wonderful people in my life like you. You are in my prayers. I love you, and Jesus does too. Never stop seeking God's face. He longs to be closer to you.

3)
God has opened my eyes to a lot of things lately and giving me discernment on many things in my life. And I just thank Him for disciplining me.

Sunday's message from proverbs 22:6 "Train up a child in the way that he should go and when he grows old he will not depart from it" WOW, even though I'm not biologically a parent, every youth that I'm involved with look up to me as a parent. I'm still part of their growth and development especially our youth group. I know the church expects a lot from them, but only a few make an effort to reach them. We really need to pray for our youth group. I have been at this church since 2000 and over the years, there has been a drastic change within our youth, as a matter of fact at this church as a whole. This is something that has been on my heart for a long time, because I seriously pondered leaving this church, due to the lack of food. Right now I'm at a point where I'm starving, I'm so hungry for God but I'm not being fed. There isn't any spiritual growth here; we have gotten too comfortable too satisfied with where we are as a church but in reality WE ARE IN BONDAGE! The devil is happy with us right now. Because here is a church with true believers and non -believers that are satisfied with where they are that they don't even know that they are in bondage. Are youth are dying, people in church are still leaving with heavy burdens, and the same young lady who goes up at altar call every Sunday still has a demon in her and no one is helping her, no one is casting that demon out of her. We do praise and worship but people don't know what praise and worship is. I see why are youth are the way they are. They are a direct replica of our adults. And those of us who are hungry for God either end up leaving or become stagnant. Salvation is a continuing process. We need to pray for the Salvation and deliverance of our church.

4)

At this time the Lord has called me to a 40 day fast in which I started about two weeks ago. It's so amazing how He works because He told me today that Word Poets would not start until after the fast. He also told me that He would bring the disciples to me. So on that note, I'm not sure if He means that I should not have open auditions. I know He will guide me when the time comes near.

I have been writing a lot (not me but by the Holy Spirit) mainly on the end times. Two nights ago a friend of mine told me that God told them to tell me that I am being called into the prophetic ministry. God is just so awesome because I didn't tell my friend anything about what I'm doing. And God has been dealing with me in regards to walking out into my calling.

This has been such a great season for me because I'm realizing a lot about myself and what I need to die to. All my desires, all my ambitions, all my goals in life are nothing but VANITY. None of it matters. Food, clothes, none of that matters. As I continue to feed on every word of God, more of Maeva dies. I have even surrendered Arts of Color Productions to God. It's His now, my family is His now, my desires are His now, all I have is His word.

Please keep me in prayer as my body becomes weak daily, but my mind has not, my spirit has not. Please pray that the results of this fast brings about healing, broken chains and restoration to God's people.

Maèva
Under the Influence

Psalm 9-1-1
(Most of the text is adapted from Psalm 91 New Living Translation. Tyndale.)

Those who abide in the shelter of the Most High
Shall find rest in the shelter of the Almighty
This I declare of the Lord
For He is my refuge, my place of safety
He is my God and I am trusting Him
He will rescue from every trap
He will protect me from the fatal plague
He will shield me with His wings
He will shelter me with His feathers
His faithful promises are my armor and protection

I am not afraid of the terrors of the night nor fear the dangers of the day
Nor do I dread the plague that stalks in darkness nor the disaster that strikes at midday
Though thousands fall at my side
Though ten thousands are dying around me
These evils will not touch me
But I will see it with my own eyes
I will see how the wicked are punished

See, I have made the Lord my refuge
I've made the Most High my shelter
No evil will conquer me
No plague will come near my dwelling
For He has ordered His angels to protect me wherever I go
They hold my hand to keep me from striking my foot on a stone

Not by might, not by my own strength but by the Spirit
I am trampling down lions and poisonous snakes
I crush fierce lions and serpents under my feet

The Lord says, " I will rescue those who love me
I will protect those who trust in my name
When they call on me I will answer
I will be with them in trouble
I will rescue them and honor them
I will satisfy them with long life
And give them my salvation."

Wake Up Call

I know all the things you do
And that you have a reputation too for being alive
But you're living a lie
You're dead
Now wake up
It's time to wake up
Strengthen what little remains
For even what is left
Is at the point of death
Your deeds are far from right in the sight of God
You've turned away and gone astray
Following your own selfish desires
Forgetting what the Lord requires
Love your neighbor as yourself and love Me with all your heart
And all your mind and all your strength
Don't be deceived by these false prophets and
Their lies of religions and self-gratification
Spiritual warfare is what's ruining our nation
Forget your situation
Its about revelation, the end times are here
And the Messiah's return is near
Go back to what you heard and believed at first
Hold to it firmly and turn to God again
Unless you do
He will come upon you
Like a thief in the night
So you better get right
This message that I bring is not my own
Renew your thinking
Renew your mind
This world that we live in is not our kind
Wake up
It's time to wake up

Get Ready

People Get Ready
The Lord is coming
Like a thief in the night
So you better get right (2x)

The Holy Spirit speaks to us
And nurtures us, preparing us to lead the way
These are the last times and some are turning away
Going astray from what they learned at first
Following lying spirits and teachings that comes from demons
These teachers are hypocrites and liars
They pretend to be your friend
But they are already dead
Being controlled by the enemy
We need to train ourselves Spiritually
Are you ready to work hard and suffer much in order for souls to believe?
The truth, for my hope is in the living God
Who is the Savior of all people and particularly to those who seek
Teach these things to the lost and the weak
Don't let anyone think less of you because you are young
For the Word of God will come forth from your tongue
Be an example to all believers in what you teach
How you walk and how you speak
Live a life of love, faith and purity
Focus on reading the scriptures
And let the Holy Spirit lead ya
Don't neglect the spiritual gift you received
Give your complete attention to the prophecies
Throw yourself into your tasks so others will see
That the life you are living is only for the King
Stay true to what is right
And keep fighting the good fight
Don't let the lack of funds
Prevent you from being rich in action
Don't participate in the sins of others for they will be a distraction
Keep yourselves pure
Pursue a godly life
And His spirit will help you endure

People Get Ready
The Lord is coming
Like a thief in the night
So you better get right (2x)

Stay Strong

He's coming like a thief in the night
So don't be like the others who are asleep
But be alert and self controlled 'cause you belong to the King
So put on faith and love as a breastplate
And the hope of salvation as a helpmate
Encourage one another as you are doing
Build each other up; don't get caught in the ruins
In fact, respect those who work hard among you
Hold them in the highest regards too
Live in peace with one another
And don't be like Abel's brother
Warn those who are idle
Pray with the weak
Deliver His message wherever you go
He is with you continually
Be joyful always
Give thanks in all circumstances
This is His will for you
Who stay true
To the faith
Listen now and listen good
Do not put out the spirits' fire that dwells in you
Do not treat prophecies with contempt
So repent and turn way from evil deeds
For He has planted a seed
And shall grow tonight
What you thought was right
Stay away from it
Have faith for the One who called you is faithful
So break free
He is your strength, your shelter, and your safety
Keep your whole spirit, soul and body blameless
For He is coming soon and He says " I know who belong to me".

Push Yourselves

There is more to this walk that I walk
And in this talk that I talk
There's more to it
There's Truth to it
So I got to do it
You wanna get in to it
All you got to do is
Walk the walk that I walk
Talk the talk that I talk

There are 86, 400 seconds in a day
What are you doing?
Are you living the life that the Lord called you to?
Are you living the life that the Lord brought you through?
Don't you know that He chose you boo
To know His will and hear Him speak
To take His message to the lost and the weak
In the streets of the New Jerusalem
Today's youth don't recognize what's in store for them
So it's up to us to bring Christ to them
Like One Accords and Galilees
Not Sadducees and Pharisees
Who keep them blinded by religion
Our youth need to catch the vision
Let's stop all this nonsense of subdivisions
There's only one kind of Christian
Holy and Righteous
Light shinning like copper—boy
Walking in the streets with steps in order—boy
Being messengers of the Christ
Breathe Life to ya—boy
You say that you've been saved
Then prove it today
Get up and be baptized
And activate your faith.

You got to push yourself out your comfort zone
You got to push yourself if you're after His throne
There's more to life then being satisfied
There's more to life when you're serving Christ

There is more to this walk that I walk
And in this talk that I talk
There's more to it

There's Truth to it
So I got to do it
You wanna get in to it
All you got to do is
Walk the walk that I walk
Talk the talk that I talk

Mountain High

I've been to the mountaintop
I've been to the valley low
My people are destroyed
Because of what they don't know
Lack of knowledge
Is a disease
Captivating many
Causing much to bleed
Enduring the curse
Instead of accepting the blessing
Curses will continue to operate
Generation after generation
Until someone breaks and reverses it
We are dealing with a spiritual force
Is this where nature takes its course?
Lift every voice and sing
Until earth and Heaven ring
Where is your scale of trust?
Is it in the word of God?
Or our own thoughts
Theories and philosophies
Has brainwashed us dramatically
And we are forgetting our identity
For we've been created in the image of a Higher Being
So what we are experiencing?
The end of ages still draws near
As the world turns for the return of the King
So what's the point to this message that I bring?
Turn to God for there is forgiveness of sins
Free at last
Free at last
Thank God Almighty
We are free at last
Claim your victory.

ABOUT THE AUTHOR

Maèvaromynathalie Guirand Renaud (Maèva) was born on January 8th, 1983 in Port-au-Prince, Haiti and grew up in south Florida. Maèva is the Founder and Artistic Director of Arts of Color Worship Arts Institute, Inc. (formerly Arts of Color Productions) a ministry through multi-media and the performing arts. Maèva has also published *Change is Coming: Dreams Pursued, Purpose Fulfilled (2008)* and is currently working on her third book *Falling In Love Again For The Very First Time.* Maèva is a creative writer, poet, and youth advocate dedicated to bring about change in peoples' lives. Her passion is to make her writing come to life in various mediums.

For more information on bookings or to place an order please write or call:

Maèva Renaud
320 S. Flamingo Road #298
Pembroke Pines, FL 33027
Phone: (305) 297-9247
Email: maevatheartist@aol.com
Websites: www.maevatheartist.com

www.ingramcontent.com/pod-product-compliance
Lightning Source LLC
Chambersburg PA
CBHW021913040426

42447CB00007B/842